The Maui Vegetarian
Cooking With Aloha

Please see our website at:
www.themauivegetarian.com

Printed in China 2005
By Sunquest Inc.
Shanghai China
Published and created by Brian Igarta
Contact at EZEKEIL1119@aol.com
Copyrighted in 2005

And God said,
"See I have given you
every herb that yields
seed which is on the face
of all the earth, and every
tree whose fruit yields seed;
to you it shall be for food."
Genesis 1:29

International missionary society
SDA1914.org

Heleconia

Whenever hiking through the lush rainforest of the east side on Maui, many varieties of heleconia such as these grace the landscape as well as people's homes. This type of tropical flower is used for export quite frequently and is a very hardy flower, lasting several days.

This book is dedicated to Skye "Mana" DuBoyce

Straight from heaven into your Daddy's arms

Special thank you goes out to my wife; I would not have gotten this book out if it weren't for her. To everyone that I worked with during my career who cared enough to teach me. Thank you to Henry Clay Richardson and Mark Tsuchiyama for teaching me most of what I know and for having the faith in me and for the times you stuck your neck out for me.

THANK YOU EVERYONE

Kepaniwai

This beautiful stream flows in the heart of Maui bringing cool, refreshing and life-giving water for most of the residents. It is a calm retreat for visitors and locals alike.

Contents

Wailea···

···means "calm waters of the canoe maker goddess." This scenic point is taken from the south shore of Maui. Much of Maui, has sandy beaches as well as rocky shorelines. The island of Kaho'olawe is pictured on the far right.

"Aloha ia Ka po e Apau"

Our warmest greetings of aloha to you. We wanted to help people be more aware of a healthier way of living through cooking. People are always asking us what we eat, thinking that all we eat are vegetables or that we can't possibly get enough protein being vegetarian. Although most people do agree that this type of vegetarian lifestyle is "healthier," they don't understand how it can be so and how it could even be satisfying. Our answer to the food part is easy, just take a look inside this book. The questions to the nutrition aspect of being vegetarian, well, need a little more research. It is not the purpose of this book to convince you of that, but only to encourage you to seek the information and find out for yourselves how a natural, vegetarian diet can fulfill all our nutritional needs.

There are many benefits in making better choices in what we eat. These are some of the rewards realized in incorporating lots of healthful whole grains, vegetables, fruits, legumes (beans and peas), seeds and nuts:

- Weight loss
- Lowered cholesterol
- Stronger immune system
- More energy
- Lowered risk of heart disease
- Less risk of many kinds of cancers
- Less harmful to the body organs
- Clearer mind and more passive attitude
    - and the list goes on.

With these inspired recipes utilizing what is natural and good for our bodies, it is our hope that we can spark your creativity and help you to be excited about desiring a healthier lifestyle. Many of the recipes can be altered to suit your taste and/or special needs. Feel free to experiment with trying variations and maybe even creating something new!

Pineapple

Pineapple is not native to the Hawaiian islands, it was brought here in the late 1700's by Captain James Cook becoming a booming business for Hawaii by the 1880's. The symbol of a pineapple signifies a sign of welcome to many homes.

Appetizers

Artichoke Dip
Traditional Hummus
Roasted Garlic Bulbs
Brushetta
Eggplant Tart
Oriental Shumai
Stuffed Portobello Mushrooms
Olive Dip
Fresh Tomato Salsa
Pineapple Salsa

Artichoke Dip

Artichoke Dip

$1/2$ cup raw cashews

$1/2$ cup hot water

2 Tbsp. lemon juice

1   tsp. liquid aminos

1   tsp. sea salt

$1/2$ cup olive oil

$1/2$ cup seasoned breadcrumbs

$1/2$ cup onion, chopped fine

$1/2$ cup red bell pepper, diced fine

2 ounces green chiles or to taste

2 cloves garlic, minced

1 can artichokes, drained and chopped

"parmesan," to taste

①Place cashews and water in blender and process until smooth.

②Add in lemon juice, liquid aminos and salt, blending all ingredients well. Slowly add in the olive oil. Set this mixture aside.

③On medium-high heat, saute onions, red bell pepper, chiles, and garlic in a tablespoon of oil. When onions have become transparent, add in the artichokes and saute for a few more minutes.

④Add in the blended mixture and stir to combine and heat thru.

⑤Transfer to an oven-proof baking dish and sprinkle with "parmesan" or top with the bread crumb mixture. Bake at 350* just until browned. Served with sliced and toasted bread of your choice.

Bread crumb topping: Mix $1/4$ cup seasoned bread crumbs with 2 Tbsp. olive oil to produce a mixture that sticks together. Sprinkle over artichoke dip and sprinkle paprika over that. Bake as directed in recipe.

Hummus and Roasted Garlic Bulbs

Traditional Hummus

1-16 oz can garbanzo beans, rinsed and drained
juice of one lemon
1 clove garlic
1 tsp. sea salt
2 Tbsp. flaxseed oil
4 oz. tahini

①In a food processor add all ingredients and process until smooth, scraping down sides as needed. Use this recipe as a great spread for sandwiches. To use as a dip for crackers or vegetable sticks, add 2 ounces of water to the recipe to thin out the mixture.

For variations, try adding one or more of the following: 1/3 cup sun dried tomatoes, 1/3 cup roasted bell pepper, 1/3 cup fresh cilantro or basil.

Roasted Garlic Bulbs

whole garlic bulbs
olive oil

①Cut off tops of garlic bulbs.
②Place each bulb in a shallow baking pan or dish that has been coated with oil. Pour some oil on the tops of garlic as well.
③Roast in oven at 350* until it becomes soft, about 25-30 minutes.

To serve: Squeeze out garlic from the skins into small individual serving dishes with more warmed olive oil and serve with slices of warm bread.

Brushetta

Brushetta

3 fresh whole tomatoes, diced

$1/2$ medium red onion , chopped fine

2 cloves garlic, minced

1 bunch fresh parsley, chopped fine

$1/4$ red or yellow bell pepper

1 Tbsp. capers

2 Tbsp. olive oil

1 Tbsp. liquid aminos

seasoned salt, to taste

①Combine tomatoes, onion, garlic, bell pepper and parsley in a bowl.

②Add capers, olive oil, liquid aminos and salt, mixing thoroughly.

③Chill for several hours before serving. Serve on sliced and toasted baguettes.

Eggplant Tart

Eggplant Tart

1- 2 round eggplant, cut into $1/4$" thick slices
2 yellow zucchini, sliced thin
5 fresh tomatoes, diced small
$1/2$ medium onion, diced fine
$3/4$ cup basil pesto
2 Tbsp. olive oil

①Saute eggplant in 1 Tbsp. olive oil until it has slightly softened. Place eggplant in a separate dish.

②Reheat the pan and add another tablespoon of olive oil. Saute the onion until browned and then add the tomatoes. Continue to saute until the water from the tomatoes has dissipated. Remove from heat and set aside.

③In a baking dish, place the first layer of eggplant thoroughly covering the bottom of the dish so that there are no spaces. Next, layer the onion/tomato mixture. Spread pesto onto the tomato mixture, then the sliced zucchini.

④Repeat layers in the same order, pressing down firmly.

⑤Bake in 350* oven for 30 minutes.

⑥Cool, then cut into slices, lay on a small plate and garnish with a sprig of basil.

Oriental Shumai

Oriental Shumai

1/2 cup onion

1 Tbsp. garlic, minced

sesame oil

2 tsp. ginger, grated

1/2 cup bulgur wheat

1 1/4 cups water

1/2 cup teriyaki marinade

1 1/2 cup nappa cabbage, chopped fine

1/4 cup carrot, grated

1/4 cup green onion, chopped fine

1/4 cup water chestnuts, chopped fine

2 Tbsp. cilantro

1 Tbsp. hoisin sauce

wonton wrappers

①In a saucepan, sauté the onion and garlic in 1 Tbsp. sesame oil until tender. Add ginger and sauté for another minute. Add the bulgur and cook for about another four minutes, stirring constantly.

②Add 1 cup of the water and simmer until the bulgur has softened and absorbed most of the water.

③Add in the teriyaki sauce and continue to simmer until all the moisture is removed. Set aside to a separate bowl.

④In the same skillet, heat another tablespoon of sesame oil, saute the remaining vegetables and water chestnuts until crisp-tender.

⑤Add this mixture to the bulgur mixture and stir in the hoisin sauce.

⑥Fill each wonton wrapper with approximately a teaspoon of filling. Be sure to squeeze the air out. Use water to help seal the edges and fold in either a triangle or rectangle shape. Or you may fold it fancy by first folding into a triangle. Then bend back the corner opposite the straight edge and fold forward the two remaining corners using a dab of water to hold the corners together.

⑦In a clean skillet, heat approximately a tablespoon of sesame oil. Place prepared shumai in pan and brown evenly. When browned, reduce the heat to low and quickly pour in 1/4 cup of the water into the skillet and cover immediately, letting it steam off. Remove and place on a serving dish. Garnish with sauce and chopped green onions and toasted sesame seeds, if desired.

Sauce: You can pour over a combination of any of these: soy sauce, Thai red chili sauce, lemon juice.

Stuffed Portobello Mushrooms

Stuffed Portobello Mushrooms

8 large Portobello mushrooms
1 Tbsp. olive oil
$1/2$ medium onion, diced
4 cloves garlic, minced
$1/2$ green bell pepper, diced fine
1 stalk celery, diced fine
2 Tbsp. Italian seasoning
2 Tbsp. nutritional yeast
$1/2$ cup croutons
$1/4$ cup water
$1/2$ cup butternut squash, cooked and diced

①Rinse and pat dry mushrooms. Rub oil on mushrooms and sear on both sides in a hot skillet until it becomes tender. Set aside to cool.
②Heat oil in skillet to medium high and add onion, garlic, bell pepper, celery, Italian seasoning and nutritional yeast. Cook until vegetables are tender.
③In a small bowl, place croutons and just enough water to soften them, gently stir in with the vegetable mixture and the diced squash. Set aside.
④Take the mushrooms and cut in half. Then cut a slit into the middle, do not cut through, but just enough to form like a pita pocket. Place enough of the mixture into each pocket and pat down so that stuffing is placed evenly within the pocket. Place pockets on a pan and place in oven just to heat thru.
You may top with red sauce and a sprinkling "parmesan," if desired.

Olive Dip

Olive Dip

2 cans black olives
1-16 oz jar green olives, pitted
8 oz. pepperocini peppers, stems and seeds removed
4-6 cloves fresh garlic
olive oil , to desired consistency

①Combine all ingredients in a food processor until chopped very fine.
②Stir in the olive oil to desired consistency. Store in refrigerator in a
glass jar and top with a layer of olive oil. Keeps for up to two weeks.

Tomato and Pineapple Salsa

Fresh Tomato Salsa

4 ripe tomatoes, diced medium
1/2 onion, diced fine
3-5 cloves of fresh garlic, minced
1-4 oz. can green chiles
1 can diced tomato
jalapenos, diced fine

2 Tbsp. fresh cilantro, chopped
1 green bell pepper, diced fine
2 Tbsp. green onion, chopped fine
1 Tbsp. cumin
2 tsp. tomato paste
sea salt, to taste

①Combine all ingredients, mix well. Refrigerate and let stand for an hour or so before serving. You may also combine all ingredients in a food processor for more of a "saucy" salsa.
Variations: Add a 1 cup of black beans that have been rinsed and drained and/or a cup of fresh or frozen corn.

Pineapple Salsa

1 fresh pineapple, remove core and diced fine
1/2 medium red onion, diced fine
1 whole red bell pepper, diced fine
2-3 cloves garlic, minced
1 tsp. cumin
1 tsp. paprika
1 tsp. red pepper
Juice of one lemon or lime
1/4 sweet thai chili sauce
jalapenos, to taste
sea salt, to taste

①Combine all ingredients in a plastic bowl. Refrigerate and let stand for an hour or so before serving.

Taro

Early Polynesian seafarers brought this food staple to Hawaii aboard their sailing canoes. Taro is rich in calcium, riboflavin, iron and thiamin. It has no cholesterol and almost no fat. Taro is the healthiest of foods, often given to babies as their first food. It is also used medicinally for many ailments. The cut portion of the haha (stem) can be rubbed on insect bites and rashes, the thin skin from around the stem helps to clot blood when wrapped around a wound, and po'i (the cooked and pounded bulb) can be used to soothe burns.

Soups & Curries

Puerto Rican Soup

Lentil Soup

Lentil Curry

Creamy Corn and Broccoli Chowder

Tomato-Spinach Stew

Lentils with Pasta

Coconut Curry

Spicy Thread Soup

Indian Curry Soup

Yam Noodle Soup

Chef's Note: For soups I like to infuse oil with herbs and spices. This means heating the oil and seasonings on very low tempetures so the oil carries the flavor. Most chefs like to add their fresh herbs at the end. For a smoother, more full-body flavor I put mine in from the get go.

Puerto Rican Soup

Puerto Rican Soup

2 cloves garlic, minced
1 small onion, chopped
1 green bell pepper, chopped
2 stalks celery, chopped (include leaves)
1 bunch cilantro chopped
3 Tbsp. annatto-infused oil*
3 potatoes, cubed

1 can kidney beans
1- 12 oz. can tomato sauce
4 cups water
1 cup elbow macaroni, cooked
fresh oregano, chopped
salt, to taste

①Saute garlic, onion, bell pepper, celery and cilantro in oil until softened.
②Add tomato sauce and water, stirring well to combine.
③Add in the kidney beans and potatoes.
④Add in salt and oregano (about 3 Tbsp fresh oregano or 1 Tbsp. dried).
Simmer until potatoes are nearly soft.
⑤Add in the cooked macaroni (or pasta of your choice) and cook about another
15 minutes until macaroni is heated thru and potatoes are tender.

*More commonly known as "achiote" in the islands.

Chef's Note: If achiote is unattainable, infuse 2 Tbsp paprika in ½ cup oil, use this on any tomato base dish and see food magic happen.

<u>Lentil Soup</u>

Lentil Soup

1 ½ cups dry lentils

1 Tbsp. olive oil

1 small onion, diced

3 cloves garlic, minced

½ stalk celery, chopped small

1 carrot, chopped small

½ green bell pepper, diced

1 tomato, diced

1 tsp. dried oregano

½ tsp. thyme

½ cup apple juice

1 Tbsp. tomato paste

water

sea salt, to taste

①Sort and rinse lentils. Place in a pot of water and cook until tender. Drain and set aside.

②Heat oil in a saucepan and add the onion, celery, carrot, and garlic. Saute until browned.

③Add the bell pepper, tomato and herbs and saute for 3 more minutes.

④Add in the apple juice, tomato paste and enough water to cover the mixture.

⑤Add in the lentils and more water to cover the lentils. Simmering until heated through.

⑥Add in salt to taste just before serving.

Lentil Curry

2 cloves garlic, chopped
1 medium onion, diced
2 Tbsp. olive oil
1 cup carrots, diced small
2 stalks celery, diced
1 Tbsp. curry seasoning
1 vegetable bouillon
1/4 cup honey

1/4 cup apple butter
1/2 cup dry lentils, sorted and rinsed
1/2 can coconut milk
2 cups water
2 cups potatoes, rinsed and diced
salt, to taste
cornstarch/water slurry, to thicken sauce

①Saute onion and garlic in a small amount of olive oil until softened.
②Add carrots and celery and continue to saute for another minute.
③Add curry seasoning, bouillon, honey, apple butter, coconut milk, lentils and water, bringing to a boil. Turn down heat and continue to simmer for an additional 30 minutes, until lentils are nearly softened.
④Add potatoes and cornstarch/water slurry mixture, bringing to a boil once again. Turn down heat to a simmer, cooking until potatoes are done.
Serve over basmati or couscous.

Creamy Corn and Broccoli Chowder

1 Tbsp. olive oil
1 med. onion, diced
3 cups water
1 1/4 cups instant mashed potatoes
2 cups cut broccoli

1 1/2 cups frozen kernel corn
1/4 tsp. salt
1/4 tsp. garlic powder
1/2 tsp. parsley flakes
1 cup rice milk

①Heat oil in saucepan, cook onion till softened.
②Add water, heat till boiling, stir in potatoes; cook 1 minute stirring constantly.
③Stir in broccoli, corn, salt, garlic powder and parsley flakes. Heat to boiling. Reduce heat to low simmer about 10 minutes, stirring occasionally until vegetables are tender.
④Stir in rice milk. Cook 3-4 minutes longer.

Tomato-Spinach Stew

2 medium red potatoes, washed and diced
1 medium onion, diced
2 cloves garlic, minced
1 can stewed or diced tomatoes
$1/2$ lb. fresh green beans, cut
$1/4$ cup water mixed with 2 Tbsp. cornstarch (to make a slurry)
1- 10 oz. pkg. frozen spinach
olive oil
1 Tbsp. curry seasoning
sea salt, to taste

①Saute garlic and onion in pot with little bit of olive oil.
②Add the diced potatoes and continue to saute until onions are tender. Add the green beans and seasonings, stirring until green beans are softened.
③Add the can tomatoes and spinach along with the water/cornstarch slurry, bringing to a boil. Reduce heat to a simmer until potatoes are tender. Serve with brown rice or whole wheat tortillas.

Lentils with Pasta

$3/4$ cup dry lentils, sorted and rinsed
$1/2$ cup minced onion
$1/2$ cup carrots, chopped small
$1/2$ cup finely chopped fresh mushrooms
1 cup tomato sauce
2 $1/2$ cups vegetable broth*
$1/2$ cup dry alphabet pasta

① In a saucepan, combine lentils, onion, carrot, mushroom, tomato sauce and broth. Cover and simmer about 45 minutes or till lentils are tender.
② Add the dry pasta. Cover and simmer 10 minutes or until pasta is tender, stirring occasionally.
*Or 2 $1/2$ cups water and 1 vegetable bouillon.

Coconut Curry

Coconut Curry

3 cloves garlic
3" piece ginger
2 Tbsp. sesame oil
1/2 tsp. Thai red or green curry paste
1 can coconut milk
2 Tbsp. hoisin sauce
3 stalks lemongrass, leaves removed
1/4 cup coconut syrup
Cornstarch slurry

①Sauté garlic, ginger and lemongrass in sesame oil for 4-5 minutes on low heat.
②Add coconut milk, hoisin sauce and syrup. Simmer for 15-20 minutes.
③Strain mixture to remove garlic, ginger and lemongrass.
④Return sauce to low heat , simmering until it is time to add cornstarch
⑤Next the vegetables.

1 cup potatoes, large cubed
1/2 cup cauliflower, cut into floweret's
1/2 cup broccoli, cut into floweret's
1/2 cup carrots, cut into 1/4 " pieces at angle
1 medium onion, diced large
1/2 each red and green bell peppers, large diced

①Parboil carrots, onion and broccoli to soften. Add in potatoes and zucchini last.
②When all vegetables are tender, drain out the water and combine the vegetables with the sauce.
Serve over hot basmati or jasmine rice.

Spicy Thread Soup

Spicy Thread Soup

Soup stock:

1 onion, sliced quartered
2 carrot, peeled and cut in chunks
2" piece ginger, smashed
2 stalks lemongrass, green removed and white part smashed
4 cloves garlic, peeled and skins removed
1 Tbsp. sesame oil

①In a large pot, heat sesame oil.
②Add in the vegetables and brown for a few minutes.
③Add 1 quart water and bring to a boil.
④Reduce heat to a simmer for 20 minutes. While simmering prepare noodles and vegetables.

½ lb. soba (Japanese buckwheat) noodles
1 pkg. vermicelli noodles (Oriental rice noodles)
2 carrots, finely shredded
1 medium zucchini, finely shredded
½ onion, sliced fine
kim chee and green onions, for garnish (if desired)

①Cook noodles as directed on package. Drain, rinse with cool water and set aside.
②Strain the vegetables from the stock and replace the stock to the pot.
③Add in 1 Tbsp. sea salt and 1 tsp. chicken-style seasoning (opt). Add more salt, if needed.
④Add in the noodles and sliced vegetables and simmer for 5 minutes.
⑤Place noodles and soup to individual serving bowls and garnish with kim chee and diced green onion.

Indian Curry Soup

Indian Curry Soup

1 Tbsp. olive oil

1 medium eggplant

1 zucchini

1 carrot

4 cloves garlic, minced

$1/2$ tomato, seeded

2 Tbsp. Indian curry spice

2 cups coconut milk

3 cups soup stock

$1/4$ cup cilantro

cornstarch/water

sea salt

①Dice eggplant, zucchini and carrot very fine.

②In a large saucepan, heat oil on high heat. Add in the diced vegetables, garlic and tomato. Cook until tender, about 2 minutes.

③Add in the curry spice. Reduce the heat and continue stirring for another minute. Cook out spices at this point.

④Add in the coconut milk and soup stock, bringing to a simmer for 10 more minutes.

⑤Add in the cilantro. Combine cornstarch and water to make a slurry and add to soup to thicken.

⑥Add salt to taste. Serve hot with warm slices of pita bread.

Yam Noodle

Yam Noodle Soup

1 can yam noodle

1 package cooked udon

2 cups soup stock (from spicy noodle recipe)

1 Tbsp. sesame oil

1 bulb ginger

1 stalk lemongrass

2 Tbsp. soy sauce

①Blanch noodles for a few minutes until loosened. Drain and set aside.

②In a sauce pot, heat the oil over low heat.

③Add the ginger and lemongrass and infuse for about four minutes.

④Add the soup stock and adjust with salt.

⑤Strain out the ginger and lemongrass and discard. Add both noodles to the strained soup stock and serve hot. Season with soy sauce and sliced green onions if desired.

Plumeria

Named after Charles Plumier, a seventeenth-century French botanist. Commonly known as Frangipani, they have a marvelous perfume which seems more intense on balmy, warm nights. Here in Hawaii they are used to make beautiful and fragrant floral garlands or "lei".

Entrees

BBQ Meatloaf
Vegetarian Meatloaf
Bulgur Tacos
Black Bean Patties
Artichoke Patties
Stuffed Green Bell Peppers
Corn Tamale Bake
Green Rice
Polenta Loaf
Basic Gluten
Beef-Style Broccoli
Beef-Style Tomato
Chinese Steamed Buns
Vegetable Couscous and
Chick Peas
Couscous Burrito
Saffron Risotto
Puerto Rican-Style Rice
Water Chestnut Fried Rice
Spanish Rice
Garlic Fried Rice
Vegetable Paella

Barbeque Meatloaf

Barbeque Meatloaf

1 can garbanzo beans, drained
2 cups cooked brown rice
1 vegetable bouillon
1 cup breadcrumbs
$1/2$ cup walnuts, chopped
2 Tbsp. olive oil
$1/4$ tsp. celery salt
$1/4$ tsp. seasoned salt
$1/2$ tsp. sage

1 tsp. parsley flakes
1 tsp. hickory seasoning (opt.)
1 Tbsp. beef-style seasoning
2 Tbsp. liquid aminos
2 cloves garlic, minced fine
1 small onion, minced
1 carrot, grated
$1/4$ cup barbeque sauce
$1/2$ cup rice or nut milk

①Mash garbanzo beans or use a food processor. Add in remaining ingredients. And mix thoroughly. If necessary, add more milk to make a thick consistency that will stick together.
②Flatten mixture into a loaf pan and spread additional barbeque sauce in a thick layer over the top. Bake at 350* for 45 minutes.

Vegetarian Loaf

1 $1/2$ cups bread crumbs
2 cups cooked brown rice
1 cup cooked lentils (from Lentil Soup recipe)
1 cup chopped walnuts (very fine)
1 cup rice milk
2 Tbsp. flax seed meal
1 Tbsp. chopped parsley or 1 tsp. dried parsley
1 small onion, chopped or $1/2$ cup dried onion
1 tsp. sea salt
2 Tbsp. beef-style seasoning
2 Tbsp. liquid aminos

①Combine all ingredients and mix thoroughly.
②Place in a loaf pan and bake for 50 minutes in a 350* oven. Serve with ketchup or gravy and a side of mashed potatoes or potato wedges.

Bulgur Tacos

Bulgur Tacos

1 Tbsp. olive oil
$1/2$ medium green bell pepper
1 Tbsp. chopped garlic
1 medium onion, diced small
1 tomato, diced small
1 tsp. cumin
1 tsp paprika

1 tsp savory
1 tsp. chili powder
2 cups bulgur
1- 8 oz. can tomato sauce
water, approx. 1 $1/2$ cups
$1/2$ tsp. salt

①Cook onion, bell pepper, tomato and garlic in olive oil over medium-high heat until all vegetables are browned and tender.
②Add cumin, paprika and chili powder and stir to cook off the spices.
③Add in the bulgur, stirring to coat in the mixture.
④Add in the tomato sauce, water and salt. Bring to a boil, stirring constantly. Reduce to a simmer and allow bulgur to soften and absorb the liquid, about 20 minutes.

Garnish with homemade avocado salsa or diced fresh tomatoes, sliced avocado, sliced black olives, pimiento cheese, shredded lettuce, etc.

Black Bean Patties

Black Bean Patties

1 can black beans or 8 oz. dry black beans, cooked
1 Tbsp. chopped garlic
$1/2$ green bell pepper, chopped fine
1 Tbsp. cumin
$1/2$ onion, chopped fine
2 Tbsp cilantro, chopped
1Tbsp green onion minced
$1/4$ cup bread crumbs
1 Tbsp. chili powder
flour
①Combine all ingredients in a food processor (or mash with a potato masher or fork) until it binds. Add in a little flour at a time, if necessary.
②Form into patties and use more flour, if needed, to coat the patties.
①Brown in olive oil in skillet over medium heat. Top with avocado salsa.

Artichoke Patties

2 cups cooked garbanzo beans
2 cloves garlic, minced
$1/4$ cup onion
1 Tbsp. olive oil
8 oz. can artichokes (not marinated)
1 tsp. Dijon mustard
$1/4$ cup dill pickle, diced fine or relish (opt.)
Salt, to taste
$1/2$ cup bread crumbs
1 Tbsp. flour

①In a food processor add beans, garlic, onion, oil, artichokes, mustard and pickles.
②Blend until the beans are well mixed, doesn't have to be smooth.
③Remove mix to a bowl and add in salt.
④Stir in the breadcrumbs and flour by hand. You should have a consistency that will hold together. Form into patties and brown in a skillet that has been lightly coated with olive oil. Great in sandwiches or as an entree, guacamole, if desired.

Stuffed Green Bell Peppers

Stuffed Green Bell Peppers

four large green bell pepper
1 Tbsp. olive oil
$1/2$ medium onion, chopped
$1/2$ red bell pepper, diced fine
3 clove of garlic, minced
1 large tomato, diced medium

1 tsp. dried Italian seasoning
$1/2$ cup cooked rice
$1/2$ cup cooked quinoa
$1/4$ cup chopped walnuts
$1/2$ cup bread crumbs
Salt, to taste

①Cut off tops of peppers leaving stem intact. Remove the seeds. Blanch in hot water till just tender, being sure not to over cook as they will break apart. Cool down with cold water immediately and set aside.

②In a fry pan, heat oil. Saute the onion and red bell pepper until browned.

③Add garlic, tomato and Italian seasoning and continue to saute for about 5 more minutes.

④Remove this mixture and place into a bowl with remaining ingredients and mix well.

⑤Fill the green peppers with mix, arranging them in a baking dish or pan. Spoon red sauce over tops. Bake at 350* for 45 minutes.

(Photo is shown served with sundried tomato and basil couscous).

Corn Tamale and Green Rice

Corn Tamale

1/2 cup yellow cornmeal
1/2 cup instant masa
1 -17 oz. can creamed corn
1 -12 oz. can corn
1 -14 oz. can stewed or diced tomatoes
1/2 tsp. onion powder
1/2 tsp. garlic powder
1/2 tsp. salt
2 Tbsp. olive oil
3 Tbsp. cornstarch
1 -6 oz. can pitted olives, drained and sliced

①Combine all ingredients and mix well.
②Place in a glass casserole dish. Cover and bake at 350* for 45 minutes. Remove cover and finish baking until center is set. (10-15 minutes.) Serve with salsa.

Green Rice

1 Tbsp. oil
1 cup Basmati rice
4 cloves garlic, minced
1/2 tsp. cumin
2 cups vegetable stock or water sea salt, to taste
1/2 medium onion, diced small

1/2 cup frozen or fresh spinach
1/2 cup cilantro
1/2 cup Italian flat-leaf parsley
1/2 green onion

①Blend spinach, cilantro, parsley and green onion until very fine.
②In a medium saucepan, heat the oil.
③Add garlic and onion and sauté until the onion becomes translucent.
④Add cumin and stir for a couple more minutes.
⑤Add rice and coat with oil. Combine the blended green mixture and vegetable stock.
⑥Add salt to taste, simmering on low heat for 20 minutes until all water is absorbed and rice is cooked.

Polenta loaf

Polenta loaf

1/2 medium onion, chopped	1 Tbsp. oil
1 Tbsp. garlic, minced	3 cups water
1/2 green bell pepper, chopped	2 1/2 cups corn masa
1/2 cup sun dried tomatoes, chopped	salt, to taste

①In a sauce pan, heat oil, then add onions and bell pepper. Saute until vegetables are tender.

②Add the sundried tomatoes. Saute for a few more minutes then add water and salt. Bring to boil for about four more minutes then remove pot from heat.

③Add corn masa.   Pour and mix at the same time until mixture starts to pull away from sides. Add in more masa as necessary to get a very thick consistency that is barely able to be stirred.

④Spoon mixture into greased loaf pan or casserole dish, flattening down nicely and bake at 400 degrees for 20 minutes or until top is nicely browned. Set aside till completely cooled.

⑤Slice and serve with brown gravy and steamed vegetable of your choice.

Basic Gluten

1 cup spelt flour
1 cup millet flour
$1/2$ cup whole wheat flour
1 cup gluten flour
1 Tbsp. onion powder
1 tsp. garlic powder
1 tsp. sage
1 tsp. celery salt
2 tsp. sea salt
3 Tbsp. nutritional yeast
2 Tbsp. beef-style seasoning
1 Tbsp. olive oil
1 $1/4$ cup water

Combine the flours and seasoning. Add the oil and about 1 cup of the water. Stir and gradually add the remaining water until it becomes a soft dough that does not stick. Take small amount of the dough and use your hands to form into cutlet shapes. In a stock pot, fill with water, one onion cut in quarters with the skin removed and 5 cloves of garlic that has been peeled. Bring to a boil and drop in the gluten cutlets. Gently boil for 30 minutes. Drain and let cool. Use in recipe or freeze for later use.

Beef-Style Broccoli

1 cup water
1 Tbsp. soy sauce
1 Tbsp. cornstarch
1 Tbsp. ginger, minced
1 Tbsp. garlic, minced
$1/2$ tsp. raw sugar
pinch salt
2 Tbsp. olive oil
1 medium onion
4 cups broccoli
2 gluten cutlets, sliced diagonally about $1/4$-inch thick

①Combine water, soy sauce, cornstarch, ginger, garlic, sugar and salt in a bowl. Set aside.

②In a wok or fry pan, heat the oil on high heat. Add in the onion and stir-fry for 2-3 minutes. Add the broccoli and stir-fry another minute until crisp-tender. Set aside in a separate bowl.

③Heat another tablespoon of oil and quickly brown the gluten. Add in the sauce and cook until thickened. Add the vegetables back in and toss to combine. Serve with hot rice.

Beef-Style Tomato

Beef-Style Tomato

2 Tbsp. soy sauce

2 tsp. raw sugar

1 clove garlic, minced

$1/2$-inch ginger, pressed

1 Tbsp. cornstarch

2 gluten cutlets, cut into bite-sized chunks

1 Tbsp. olive oil

1 onion, cut in large chunks

1 green bell pepper, cut into bite-sized chunks

3 tomatoes, cut in chunks

2 green onion, slivered

①In a wok or large pan, heat the oil over high heat. Saute the onion and green bell pepper until crisp-tender. Set aside to another dish.

②In the same pan, brown the gluten for a minute then add the sauce and allow to thicken slightly. Add in the tomatoes and stir.

③Reduce heat to medium and add the onion and bell pepper back into the pan. Stir, cover and allow it to steam off until the tomatoes have softened and the mixture has become more liquid. Serve over steamed rice.

CHINESE STEAMED BUNS

CHINESE STEAMED BUNS

1 package dried yeast
1 cup lukewarm water
4 $\frac{1}{2}$ cups flour (half white and half whole wheat)
$\frac{1}{4}$ cup sugar
$\frac{1}{4}$ tsp. sea salt
2 Tbsp. oil (half olive and sesame)
$\frac{1}{2}$ cup boiling water
2 Tbsp. sesame seed oil

①Dissolve yeast in water. Add 1 cup of flour and mix thoroughly. Cover with cloth. Let rise 1 hour, until bubbles appear.

②Dissolve sugar , salt and sesame oil in the boiling water. Stir well. Cool until lukewarm. Pour into yeast mixture and add remaining flour.

③Knead dough on lightly floured board until smooth. Add more flour if dough is sticky. Place into extra large, greased bowl in a warm place. Cover with damp cloth. Let rise until double in bulk, about 2 hours.

④Divide into 2 portions. Remove first portion and knead 2 minutes. Repeat with second. Roll each into roll 12" long and 2" wide. Cut into 12 pieces (24 total).

Filling:

2 tbsp. sesame oil
$\frac{1}{2}$ onion
$\frac{1}{2}$ green bell pepper
1 Tbsp. garlic
$\frac{1}{2}$ stalk of celery
2 cups broccoli
$\frac{1}{4}$ cup cilantro
$\frac{3}{4}$ cup gluten patty, chopped
$\frac{1}{2}$ hoisin sauce

①Finely chop all vegetables.

②Heat oil in pan and add onion, bell pepper, celery and garlic.   Saute until browned.

③Add broccoli, gluten, cilantro and hoisin and reduce heat to low until it gels together. Remove from heat and let cool.

④Place each roll on separate square piece of wax paper or parchment paper. Cover with clean towel and let buns rise till double in bulk, about 30 minutes.

⑤Remove towel and place buns in a single layer on steamer tray. Steam, tightly covered, over briskly boiling water for 10 minutes.

Couscous with Vegetables and Chickpeas

Couscous with Vegetables and Chickpeas

4 c. water

2 c. whole wheat couscous

1 vegetable bouillon

2 Tbsp. olive oil

1 tsp. paprika

1/2 tsp. cumin

1/2 tsp. salt

1 med. onion, chopped

2 garlic cloves, minced

1/2 med. green bell pepper, chopped

1/2 med. red bell pepper, chopped

1 zucchini, chopped into 1/4 " dice

1 med. tomato, seeded and chopped

1 cup garbanzo beans, rinsed and drained

①In a medium saucepan, heat the water and bullion to boiling over high heat. Stir in the couscous. Reduce heat to a simmer and cook, covered, until the couscous is tender, about 5 minutes. Fluff the grains with a fork and let cool.

②In a skillet heat the oil add the spices and cook for one minute, stirring frequently.

③Add the onion, garlic and peppers. Cook until softened, about 3-5 minutes.

④Stir in the zucchini and tomato. Cook until slightly softened, about 3 minutes.

⑤Add the chickpeas and cook 2 minutes longer, until heated through. Mound the couscous on a large platter and top with cooked vegetables.

Couscous Burrito

1 Tbsp. oil

1/2 onion, chopped

3 cloves garlic, minced

1/2 tsp. cumin

1/2 tsp. paprika

1/4 tsp. chili powder

3 cups water

1 1/2 cups couscous

1 cup prepared salsa

1/2 cup corn

1/2 cup black beans, cooked

flour tortillas

①In a medium saucepan, heat oil and add in onion, garlic and spices. Saute until onions become transparent.

②Add in the water and bring to a boil.

③Add in the black beans and corn into boiling water and add the couscous.

④Stir and cover, then turn off heat. When couscous mixture has finished cooking, mix with the salsa. Wrap in tortillas and serve or place in baking dish and top with enchilada sauce. Heat in 350*

Saffron Risotto

1 medium onion, diced

1 clove garlic, minced

1 Tbsp. olive oil

pinch saffron

1 cup Arborio rice (riso)

1 vegetable bouillon

2 cups water

1/4 cup nut milk

salt, to taste

①Saute onion in oil until transparent.

②Add garlic and saffron, saute for another minute.

③Add rice, coating rice with mixture.

④Add vegetable bouillon and water. Cover and bring to a simmer for about 20 minutes, stirring occasionally. When done, stir in cashew milk and salt to taste. Serve warm.

Puerto Rican Rice

Puerto Rican Rice

2 Tbsp. annatto-infused olive oil

2 cloves garlic, minced

$1/2$ onion, chopped

1 cup celery, diced

1 green bell pepper, diced

1 small bunch cilantro, chopped

1 can pigeon peas or kidney beans

2 cups long-grain brown rice

2- 8 oz. cans tomato sauce

2 cups water

fresh oregano

sea salt, to taste

①Saute garlic, onion, celery and bell pepper in oil until nearly softened.

②Add in cilantro and continue to saute for another minute, stirring often.

③Add washed rice. Stir until coated.

④Add in the tomato sauce, water, salt and beans, bringing to a boil. Stir often to avoid scorching. Bring down heat to a simmer and cover. Stirring and checking every 10 minutes or so to prevent burning the bottom. Continue cooking until water is absorbed and rice is cooked thoroughly. Add in more water, if necessary.

Spanish Rice

1 Tbsp. olive oil

1 Tbsp. garlic, minced

1 medium onion, chopped

1/2 green bell pepper, diced fine

1 tomato, diced

1 vegetable bouillon

2 cups water

1 8 oz. can tomato sauce

1/4 cup fresh basil and oregano

1 Tbsp. fresh thyme

(or 1/2 tsp. each dried herbs)

1 cup long grain brown rice

①Heat oil on medium-high in saucepan. Add the garlic, onions and bell pepper till slightly softened.

②Add tomatoes, stirring till tender.

③Add in the vegetable bouillon and rice and stir so that the rice is coated with the oil and the bouillon is dissolved.

④Add water, tomato sauce and herbs, stirring and bringing to a boil. Turn heat to low and cover, simmer until done, about 30 minutes.

Garlic Fried Rice

1 Tbsp. sesame oil

2 Tbsp. chopped garlic

1/4 cup finely chopped whites from green onion bottom

3 cups cooked day-old rice

1 Tbsp. soy sauce

1 Tbsp. olive oil

1/4 cup finely sliced green onion

1 medium eggplant, diced small

①In a skillet, heat oil and add garlic and green onion bottoms.

②Saute until tender and slightly browned. Add the rice and stir-fry the rice, thoroughly coating with garlic/oil mixture.

③Add in the soy sauce, remove from heat and add remaining green onion.

Water Chestnut Fried Rice

1 Tbsp. sesame oil
$1/2$ medium onion, chopped
1 clove garlic, minced
$1/2$ cup celery, diced
1 cup frozen peas and carrots
$1/2$ can water chestnuts, diced
$1/4$ cup green onion, diced
3 cups cooked rice
vegetarian stir-fry sauce
soy sauce
sea salt

① Saute onion, garlic and celery in a small amount of oil until softened.
② Add frozen peas and carrots and water chestnuts and cook for 2 minutes more.
③ Add the cold cooked rice and break apart, mixing thoroughly with vegetable mixture. Add in stir-fry sauce, soy sauce and salt, all to taste. Garnish with green onion.

Vegetable Paella

Vegetable Paella

1 Tbsp. olive oil
$1/2$ onion, chopped fine
1 clove garlic, minced
$1/2$ green bell pepper. chopped fine
1 small tomato, chopped fine
pinch of saffron
1 sprig of fresh thyme & oregano

1 bay leaf
$1 1/2$ cups uncooked Basmati rice
$1/2$ vegetable bouillon
1 tsp. tomato paste
3 cups water
salt, to taste

Vegetables such as carrots, baby corn, zucchini, yellow squash, small diced potatoes, green beans, broccoli, cauliflower, etc.

① Saute onion, garlic and bell pepper in olive oil until softened.
② Add tomato and saffron and sauté for another minute.
③ Add herbs, bay leaf and rice, mixing and thoroughly coating the rice.
④ Combine bouillon, tomato paste and water, bringing to a boil.
⑤ Add salt and reduce heat. Cover and simmer for about 20 minutes, until nearly done. Top with blanched vegetables and continue to simmer until rice is tender. Serve with garlic-cashew sauce drizzled over paella.

Iao Needle

A natural rock pinnacle presiding over the Iao stream and surrounded by the walls of the Pu'u Kukui Crater. Once used as a natural altar, the 2,250-foot stone pillar covered in green forest.

Pasta & Noodles

Quick and Easy Red Sauce
Roasted Veggie Lasagna
Artichoke, Basil and Lemon Linguine
Zucchini Garlic Pasta
Orzo with Macadamia Nuts
Fettuccini in Saffron Cream
Pasta with Fresh Tomato and Fried Garlic
Original Pasta Salad
Oriental Noodle Salad
Chow Mein
Chow Funn

Very Quick and Easy Basic Red Sauce for any Dish

1 can cut tomatoes or stewed tomatoes
1/2 medium onion, chopped -or- 1/2 cup chopped dried onion
3 cloves garlic, minced -or- 1 Tbsp. minced dried or jar garlic
2 Tbsp. vegan pesto   1 small can tomato paste   Water, to desired consistency
3 Tbsp. Succanat or honey -or- sweetener of your choice

①Combine tomatoes, onion, garlic and pesto in a saucepan over medium heat. Use a hand blender to blend ingredients if you desire a not-so-chunky sauce.
②Add in tomato paste and water to desired consistency.
③Add in the sweetener. You may add different vegetables according to your taste. i.e. grated zucchini, diced green or red bell peppers, etc. This sauce may be left thicker and used as a pizza sauce.

Roasted Veggie Lasagna

1 medium onion
1 zucchini
1 yellow squash
1 round eggplant
mushrooms
1 red bell pepper
4 cups red sauce

Marinade:
1/4 cup olive oil
1 Tbsp. Italian seasoning
2 cloves fresh garlic, chopped
2 Tbsp. balsamic vinegar
salt, to taste
lasagna noodles, cooked

①Cook pasta according to directions given. Drain and set aside to cool.
②Place sliced onions, zucchini, yellow squash, eggplant, mushroom and red bell pepper in a bowl. Combine marinade ingredients and toss in with the vegetables until well coated.
③Place on a baking pan or dish and broil in oven on high heat. When tender, remove from oven. Allow to cool slightly.
④Separate red bell peppers and place in a plastic bag. Let it sit for a few minutes. Then remove the skin.
⑤In a lasagna pan, spoon on a layer of sauce, then pasta. Add another layer of sauce, the grilled veggies, then pasta, repeating layers. Last layer should be the sauce and you may add a layer of pimiento cheese and "parmesan" cheese. Bake in oven at 350* for 30 minutes.

Artichoke, Basil and Lemon Linguine

1 Tbsp. olive oil

1/2 onion, sliced thin

1/2 each red and yellow bell pepper, sliced thin

2 cloves garlic, minced

Small bunch fresh basil leaves, chopped

lemon juice, to taste

1 small jar marinated artichokes, chopped

1 lb. linguine, cooked according to directions on package

sea salt, to taste

①Saute garlic, onion and peppers in olive oil until softened.

②Add in lemon juice, basil and salt.

③Turn off heat and toss in marinated artichokes and seasoning.

④Add linguine and toss well to coat. Add more lemon juice and olive oil if desired. Serve immediately.

Zucchini Garlic Pasta

Zucchini Garlic Pasta

1 pkg. wagon wheel pasta
1 med. red onion, chopped
4-6 garlic cloves, minced
2 med. zucchini, halved and sliced
3 Tbsp. lemon juice
olive oil
1/2 tsp. sea salt

①Cook pasta according to directions.
②While pasta is cooking, saute onion and garlic in a little bit of olive oil, until vegetables are tender.
③Add zucchini and salt; cook till tender, about 6 minutes. Turn off heat.
④Add in the cooked and drained pasta.
⑤Add in the lemon juice and toss. Transfer to a serving dish, sprinkle with "parmesan."

Orzo with Macadamia Nuts

Orzo with Macadamia Nuts

1 lb. orzo, cooked al dente
1 Tbsp. olive oil
1/4 cup macadamia nuts, chopped fine or pine nuts
1 Tbsp. garlic, minced
small handful fresh parsley, chopped fine
"parmesan" sprinkle
salt, to taste

①Heat oil in skillet, add nuts and brown.
②Add the garlic and saute for a few more minutes.
③Add in the cooked pasta. Add in salt to taste and toss in pan for few more minutes to heat through and to combine ingredients. Place on a serving dish and garnish with the chopped parsley and "parmesan."

Fettuccini in Saffron Cream

Fettuccini in Saffron Cream

1/4 lb. fettuccini, cooked
1/2 cup coconut milk
1/2 cup rice milk
2 cloves garlic, minced
pinch of saffron
1 Tbsp. lemon juice
cornstarch, to thicken (about 3 Tbsp.)
sea salt, to taste

①In a sauce pan, place coconut and rice milks, bringing to a low boil.
②Add the garlic, and saffron, simmering for about four minutes.
③Add lemon juice.
④In a small bowl, combine cornstarch and a little water to make a thin paste. Pour this mixture into the sauce, stirring often and bringing it to a low boil once again until sauce has thickened.
⑤Add in salt to taste. Toss noodles with the sauce and combine. Sprinkle with "parmesan" and garnish. Serve immediately.

Pasta with Fresh Tomatoes and Fried Garlic

Pasta with Fresh Tomatoes and Fried Garlic

1 lb cooked penne pasta (or similar type)

8 cloves garlic sliced very thin lengthwise

$1/4$ cup fresh herbs: basil , thyme, oregano, parsley, chopped

$1/4$ cup olive oil

4 fresh tomatoes, diced

$1/4$ cup green olive, sliced (optional)

sea salt, to taste

①In a heated skillet, combine sliced garlic and herbs with olive oil on low heat. Allow to simmer for six or seven minutes.

②Add in the tomatoes and continue to simmer for another five minutes.

③Add in the green olives if desired and salt to taste.

Original Pasta Salad

Original Pasta Salad

1 pkg. pasta (rotelle, spiral, shells, etc.)
$1/4$ cup each red and green bell peppers
1 Tbsp. capers
$1/2$ cup sliced black olives
$1/4$ cup sundried tomatoes, chopped
1 small head broccoli, chopped small
1 pkg. Good Seasons dressing, prepared with olive oil and lemon juice
"Parmesan" substitute
Salt, if desired to taste

①Prepare pasta according to directions on package. Rinse with cold water and set aside.
②Combine bell peppers, capers, olives, sundried tomatoes and broccoli. Add dressing, then toss in a large bowl with pasta. Refrigerate. Before serving, add more olive oil if necessary, sprinkle with "parmesan" and toss. Or you may use the oil that the sun dried tomato is packed in to toss into the pasta.

Oriental Noodle Salad

Oriental Noodle Salad

1 -8 oz. pkg. soba (buckwheat) noodles

1 -8 oz. pkg. somen noodles

1 small pkg. bean thread noodles

1 Tbsp. sesame oil

1 tsp. fresh orange peel

1/2-inch piece ginger

2 cloves garlic

1/2 red onion, thinly sliced

1/4 red bell pepper, thinly sliced

4 mushrooms thinly sliced

1/2 zucchini, sliced 1/4" thick at an angle

1/2 yellow squash, sliced 1/4" at an angle

1 Tbsp. chopped cilantro

1 Tbsp. tahini

1 Tbsp. soy sauce

1/2 Tbsp. Hoisin sauce

chopped green onion and toasted sesame seeds, for garnish

①Cook noodles as directed on package. When done, combine in a large bowl and set aside.

②Heat sesame oil in pan on high heat. Add orange peels and brown.

③Add the ginger and garlic, cook two more minutes.

④Add onion, bell pepper, mushrooms, zucchini, and squash. Stir-fry the vegetables over high heat.

⑤Reduce heat and add the noodles, cilantro, tahini, soy sauce and hoisin sauce. Stir to combine and replace to a serving dish.

Sprinkle with the green onion and sesame seeds, if desired.

Author's Note: For a fresher and healthier entree, slice your vegetables as thin as possible and leave it raw. The above dish is especially delicious when done in this fashion.

Chow Mein

Chow Mein

2 pkg. chow mein noodle

1 Tbsp. sesame oil

1 Tbsp. fresh garlic, minced

1/2 onion, sliced thin

1 carrot, julienne

1/4 head cabbage, chopped 1/2" wide

1 stalk celery , cut on bias

1/2 cup straw mushrooms, sliced

pinch of Chinese Five Spice

2 Tbsp. soy sauce

green onion, chopped

chopped nori

①Heat sesame oil in a large skillet or wok on high heat. Add in the garlic, onions, carrot, cabbage and celery and stir-fry for 3 minutes.

②Add in the mushrooms and spice. Stir-fry for another minute.

③Add in the noodles, stirring to combine and heat noodles through. Drizzle the soy sauce over the noodles, again stirring.

④Remove from heat and replace to a serving dish. Garnish with chopped green onion and nori.

Chow Funn

Chow Funn

1 lb. Chow Funn noodles

1 Tbsp. sesame oil

1 tsp. garlic, chopped

1 tsp. ginger, minced

1/4 onion, julienne

1 carrot julienne

1/2 cup green onion, chopped 1"

1/2 small nappa cabbage, sliced fine

mung bean sprouts handful

soy sauce to drizzle

Using either dry or fresh noodles, dry noodles need to be cooked as for fresh just needs to be warmed under hot water. When using dry noodle cook as normal but make sure to rinse of all starch that comes of noodle. Then set aside.

①In a skillet heat oil, add ginger garlic saute for one minute then add white onion cook for another minute, then add carrots and cabbage and just wilt it.

②Then take out and add to noodles, at this time while mix is still hot add sprouts and green onion. And drizzle with soy sauce. This dish does not have to be eaten hot it can be room temperature and still be tasty

Painted Eucalyptus

As beautiful as they are strong. The reddish brown bark of these trees tend to peel off exposing the green fleshy part and leaving the tree with a painted effect.

Vegetables

Carrot Wakame Salad
Cucumber Salad
Breaded Cauliflower
Herb Roasted Potatoes
Broiled Eggplant
Yams and Sweet Potato
Tiki with Tri Pesto
Swiss Chard
Kale

Carrot Wakame Salad

Carrot Wakame Salad

3 medium carrots
½ cup dried wakame seaweed

Dressing:

¼ cup fresh mint leaves	2 Tbsp. plum sauce
1 clove garlic	1 tsp. ginger
1 Tbsp. sesame oil	1 Tbsp. fresh basil
2 Tbsp. lemon juice	½ cup olive oil

①Soak seaweed in water until softened.
②Peel carrots, then slice very thin. You may use the vegetable peeler instead. Combine the drained seaweed and sliced carrots in a bowl and set aside.
③Blend all dressing ingredients except the olive oil, until smooth. While blending, slowly add the olive oil until thickened. Add sea salt to taste.
④Toss the dressing with the seaweed and carrots. Serve immediately or refrigerate and serve cool.

Cucumber Salad

Cucumber Salad

2 cucumbers
1 carrot
1 tomato
¼ red onion

Dressing:

½ cup cilantro
¼ cup fresh mint leaves
1 Tbsp. lime concentrate or juice of 1 lime
1 tsp. sesame oil
1 Tbsp. sweet thai chili sauce
2 cloves garlic
1 Tbsp. ginger
½ cup olive oil

①Julienne cucumbers and carrots very fine or use a mandolin slicer. Remove seeds from the tomato and slice fine. Sliver red onions. Combine and toss in a bowl. Set aside.
②In a blender, combine all dressing ingredients except olive oil and blend until smooth. Add in the olive oil and blend until thickened.
③Toss the dressing with the prepared vegetables and serve or refrigerate and serve cool.

Breaded Cauliflower

Breaded Cauliflower

1 head cauliflower
¼ cup seasoned bread crumbs
1 Tbsp. garlic powder
1 Tbsp. nutritional yeast
2 Tbsp. olive oil
salt, to taste

①Remove and discard stem from cauliflower and cut into bite-size pieces.
②Place cut cauliflower into a pot of boiling water until just tender, about 8-10 minutes. Drain and set aside.
③In a separate bowl, combine bread crumbs, garlic powder, nutritional yeast, and salt. Add in the oil last and mix well till it becomes a crumbly mixture. Toss in the cooked cauliflower to coat and place in a baking dish.
④Broil in oven until just browned and serve.

Roasted Potato

Roasted Potato

12 Red or Yukon gold potato
2 tsp. diced garlic
1/3 cup olive oil
¼ cup fresh herbs: rosemary, oregano, basil, thyme, parsley
1 tsp. paprika
salt, to taste
1 Tbsp. flour

①Cut potato into wedges and place in a pot of boiling water. Cook until tender. Drain well and set aside.
②In a large bowl add garlic, oil, herbs, paprika, and salt. Mix well and toss into the potatoes, coating well.
③Sprinkle flour over potatoes and bake in a preheated oven at 400 degrees until browned.

Broiled Eggplant

1 large, firm eggplant
¼ cup olive oil
1 handful chopped fresh basil
2 Tbsp. nutritional yeast
2 Tbsp. soy sauce or liquid aminos
2 tsp. minced garlic

①In a bowl, combine and mix all ingredients except eggplant.
②Slice eggplant ¼ inch thick and dip pieces into the sauce or brush the sauce on.
③Place onto a baking pan and broil until nicely browned. Turn over with a spatula and continue to broil until this side is browned too. Be careful not to burn as the eggplant cooks quickly. Serve immediately.

Yams and Sweet Potato

Pictured here are three different types of yams and sweet potato: Molokai sweet potato (purple), orange-flesh yams and white-fleshed "butter" sweet potato. These have been baked and prepared the same way you would with a regular potato and shown with a different presentation that will make any plate look more attractive.

Swiss Chard

1 bunch Swiss Chard
1 Tbsp. olive oil
1 Tbsp. fresh basil, chopped
1 tsp. garlic, minced
soy sauce

①Rinse leaves and chop into slightly large bite-size pieces.
②In a pan, heat the oil, garlic and basil.
③Add in the chard and saute until slightly wilted. Remove from heat and drizzle soy sauce. Serve immediately.

Kale

1 bunch kale
¼ cup sesame oil
liquid aminos
roasted sesame seeds
"parmesan" sprinkle

①Remove stem and vein from the kale leaf by folding in half and slicing it out. Tear leaves into bite-size pieces and rinse well.
②Steam the kale for just a few minutes. Color should remain bright green but should wilt just slightly, keeping the kale as close to raw as possible. Drain and place on a serving dish.
③Heat the sesame oil in a small saucepan until it just begins to smoke. Carefully drizzle the oil over the steamed kale.
④Drizzle liquid aminos and sprinkle with the sesame seeds. Top with "parmesan" and serve immediately.

Tiki with Tri Pesto

Tiki with Tri Pesto

sundried tomato
yellow tomato pesto
basil pesto

To make yellow tomato pesto, cut fresh yellow tomatoes in half and coat with garlic, herbs and oil. Place on a sheet pan and slow dry them in oven or use a food dehydrator. Place the dried tomatoes in a blender and add a little oil at a time till smooth. Add salt to taste. (consistency should be like that of sundried tomatoes.)

To make the "tiki": use an empty soup can or any type of cylindrical or even rectangle tall container. Grease the inside using olive oil and make sure you have something handy to push it out.

Layer ingredients as follows:

A slice of cooked yam
Diced artichoke hearts
Sliced and roasted red bell pepper
Cooked and sliced yellow squash
Mashed and blended together, garbanzo beans and ripe avocado
Another slice of cooked yam
Top with a garnish of your choice. Here we used mixed baby greens.

Arrange on a plate and garnish the sides of the tiki with alternating sundried tomatoes, the yellow tomato pesto and the basil pesto. Serve.

Wa`a

These canoe racers of fiberglass, are a far cry from what their predecessors were once made of, which was koa wood. Each island has many different teams that compete for the State finals competition called the Queen Liliuokalani, that is held on the Big Island of Hawaii

Seasonings, Sauces

Seasoned Salt
"Parmesan" Sprinkle
Indian Curry Seasoning
Mother Sauce
Garlic-Cashew Sauce
Sweet and Sour Sauce
Teriyaki Sauce
Garlic-Onion Sauce
Basic Soup Stock

Seasoned Salt

1 Tbsp. paprika
1 Tbsp. turmeric
1 Tbsp. onion powder

1 Tbsp. garlic powder
1 cup sea salt

Combine all ingredients and add mixture to sea salt in a blender or coffee grinder processing until fine. Store in an airtight glass container in a cool place.

"Parmesan" Sprinkle

1 cup almonds
2 cups nutritional yeast
sea salt, to taste

Place almonds in a food processor and process until very fine. Add in the nutritional yeast and salt and process until everything is combined well. Store in a glass jar and keep it nearby because we like to use it on just about everything. A cheesy, nutty flavor that goes well over many dishes.

Indian Curry Seasoning

1 Tbsp. paprika
1 Tbsp. garlic powder
1 Tbsp. curry powder
1 Tbsp. cumin
½ tsp. cinnamon

1 tsp. turmeric
1 tsp. nutmeg
1 tsp. ground cloves
2 Tbsp. sea salt

Combine all ingredients and blend well in a blender or coffee grinder.

Mother Sauce

A base for many sauces and dressings

½ cup raw cashews
½ hot water
1 Tbsp. sea salt
1 tsp. liquid aminos
1 Tbsp. "parmesan"
2 tsp. lemon juice
¾ cup olive oil

With this sauce being the "mother," everything starts with it:

For Caesar salad dressing: Add 2-3 cloves of garlic and 2 Tbsp. lemon juice additional to base recipe.
For Thousand Island dressing: Add ketchup or tomato paste and 1-2 Tbsp. chopped dill pickles or pickle relish.
For a creamy pesto dressing: Add basil pesto or fresh chopped basil and fresh garlic.
For a spicy Mexican-style sauce: Add chipotle peppers and garlic.

Garlic-Cashew Sauce

¼ cup cashews
1 clove of garlic
1 Tbsp. lemon juice
¼ cup water
¼ to ½ cup olive oil

Combine cashews, garlic, lemon juice and water in a blender. Blend until smooth. Slowly add in the olive oil until desired consistency. Use over paella, or as a sauce for pitas, etc.

Sweet and Sour Sauce

1 Tbsp. sesame oil
1 thumb-sized piece of ginger, crushed
½ white onion, diced large
1 stalk of celery, diced large
3 cloves of garlic, whole
1 carrot, diced large
32 oz can of pineapple juice
¼ cup raw sugar
¼ cup tomato paste
2 Tbsp. soy sauce
cornstarch, to thicken

Over medium-high heat, place sesame oil in a saucepan. Add in the ginger, onion, celery and garlic, sauté for a few minutes until slightly softened. Add the remaining ingredients and simmer for 15 minutes on low heat. Adjust flavor as needed. Once desired taste is achieved, strain the liquid out and place in the saucepan once again. Add in cornstarch/water slurry and bring to a boil to thicken the sauce.

Teriyaki Sauce

1 Tbsp. sesame oil
1 fairly large ginger root, pounded
1 whole bulb of garlic, pounded
½ cup soy sauce
1 ½ cup water

¾ cup raw sugar
1 whole lemon
1 Tbsp. crushed red pepper
cornstarch, to thicken

Heat oil in a saucepan, add ginger and garlic, sauté until softened. Add remaining ingredients and bring to a boil, stirring occasionally. Reduce heat to low and simmer for 15 minutes. Adjust taste as necessary. Strain out liquid and replace to saucepan. Add the cornstarch/water slurry and bring to a boil once again to thicken.

Garlic-Onion Gravy

½ cup olive oil
6 cloves garlic, minced
¼ of a medium onion, sliced thin
½ cup whole wheat or chickpea flour
2 Tbsp. nutritional yeast
4 Tbsp. liquid aminos

2 ½ cups water, to start
½ tsp. ground sage
Salt, to taste
1 Tbsp. fresh lemon juice
Sliced mushrooms (opt.)

On medium heat, sauté onion and garlic in oil until tender and onions are softened and transparent. Add the flour, yeast and liquid aminos to make a paste. Gradually add the water, stirring constantly. With frequent stirring, bring the gravy to a boil and allow it to thicken. Add sage, salt, lemon juice and mushrooms. Add more water to desired consistency. Make approximately 4 cups.

Basic Soup Stock

1 Tbsp. olive oil
1 whole bulb garlic
3 carrots
2 onions
3 stalks celery
5 cups water

Rinse carrots and celery, removing ends and chopping into large pieces. Remove skins from onions and rough cut. Remove skins from garlic. Heat oil in stock pot and add the garlic and vegetables. Brown the vegetables over high heat then add the water and bring to a boil. Reduce heat and simmer for 30 minutes. Strain vegetables from stock and discard vegetables.

Kealia Beach

Six miles of sand and surf make one of Maui's longest beaches perfect for an invigorating morning walk or leisurely day of beachcombing. This stretch of beach has become one of the favored spots for the nesting green sea turtles.

Salad Dressings & Cheese

Create-Your-Own Salad Dressing
Oriental Salad Dressing
Vegan Pesto
Pimiento Cheese Sauce
Garlic 'n Chive Loaf Cheese

Create-Your-Own Salad Dressing

3 parts Oil:
Pure, cold-pressed extra virgin olive oil
Walnut oil
Grape seed oil
Flaxseed oil
White or Black Truffle oil

1 part Acid:
Lemons
Limes
Fruit puree
Vinegars

Flavorings:
1-2 cloves fresh garlic
1-2" fresh ginger
½ handful of your choice fresh parsley, cilantro, basil, tarragon, rosemary, chives, mint, etc.
1 cup fresh spinach, arugula, etc.
2 Tbsp. tomato paste
Hoisin sauce
Mustards
Wasabi
Vegetable juice (from a juicer only) ¼ cup juice to 1 cup oil
Nutritional yeast
Barbecue sauce
Ground flax seed

To a blender, add your choice of oil, acid and flavorings. Blend and add sea salt to taste. To make a creamy dressing, add one or both of the following:
½ ripe avocado
¼ cup nuts (cashew, walnut, macadamia, etc.)

Basil Pesto

1 lb. fresh basil leaves, separated from stems and rinsed
1 cup raw pine nuts
½ cup peeled garlic cloves
olive oil, to desired consistency

Process until ingredients are chopped very fine and adding in oil enough to produce a wet mixture. Transfer to a glass jar topping with olive oil. Store in refrigerator for up to several weeks.

Pimiento Cheese Sauce

2 cups water
4 ounces pimientos
¼ cup raw cashews
1 tsp. sea salt
½ tsp. onion powder

¼ tsp. garlic powder
2-3 Tbsp. cornstarch
3 Tbsp. nutritional yeast
1 Tbsp. lemon juice

Combine all ingredients in a blender and blend until smooth. Cook in a saucepan over medium heat stirring constantly to avoid scorching. Use 2 Tbsp. cornstarch for sauce, and 3 Tbsp. cornstarch for a dip or spread.

Oriental Salad Dressing

½ cup hoisin sauce
½ tsp. salt
¾ cup olive oil or grape seed oil

¼ cup sesame oil
¼ cup lemon juice
3 Tbsp. raw sugar

Combine ingredients in a blender. Mix till well combined. Store in refrigerator for up to one week.

Garlic 'n Chive Loaf Cheese

Garlic 'n Chive Loaf Cheese

1 cup cold water
6 Tbsp. Emes jel
1 cup boiling water
1 cup raw cashews
2 whole bulbs roasted garlic
¼ cup chives

3 tsp. sea salt
1 tsp. onion powder
½ tsp. garlic powder
1 Tbsp. lemon juice
3 Tbsp. nutritional yeast

Soak jel in cold water in blender. Add the boiling water and blend briefly to dissolve jel. Add cashews and remaining ingredients and continue blending until smooth. Pour into a loaf pan that is lined with wax paper or plastic wrap and refrigerate until firm. Once it is firm, you may wish to store some in the freezer and keep it on hand to grate over dishes, etc.

Hibiscus

Another one of Hawaii's exotics that grow here quite abundantly. Pictured here are some hybrid ones. There are more than 200 species, only 6 being native to the Hawaiian Islands. Normally lasting for only a day, these delicate flowers are able to continue blooming if just the right weather conditions prevail.

Breakfast

Fresh Strawberry Muffins
Blueberry–Banana Muffins
Pancakes
Carob Creamy and Fruit Parfait
Apple 'n Oats Breakfast Bars
A.M. Apple Snack
Apple Butter Bars
Oats, Nuts and Raisins Breakfast Patties
Great Granola
Poi Smoothie

Strawberry Muffins

Strawberry Muffins

¾ cup quick oats, uncooked
1 cup whole wheat pastry flour
½ cup brown rice flour
½ tsp. salt
3 Tbsp. wheat germ
3 Tbsp. flax seed meal
¾ cup sucanat
¼ cup walnut oil
1 tsp. vanilla extract
1 ¼ cup almond or rice milk
2 tsp. Ener-G baking powder
1 cup fresh strawberries

①Wash and blot dry strawberries. Remove stems and dice. Set aside.
②Preheat oven to 350* and prepare muffin tins either lightly greased or lined with paper muffin cups.
③In a bowl, combine oats, pastry flour, brown rice flour, salt, wheat germ, flax seed meal and sucanat.
④In another smaller bowl or large measuring cup, combine oil, milk and vanilla.
⑤Mix in liquid ingredients to the dry and stir to mix well.
⑥Add in the baking powder and stir quickly to combine. Fold in the strawberries and immediately fill muffin cups to nearly full. Place in the oven and bake approximately 20 minutes or until toothpick inserted in center comes out clean.

Blueberry-Banana Muffins

1 cup brown rice flour
1 cup whole wheat pastry flour
1 cup spelt flour
3 Tbsp. flax seed meal
2 Tbsp. wheat germ
½ cup sucanat
½ tsp. salt
2 tsp. Ener-G baking powder
1-2 mashed banana
¼ cup walnut oil
1 ½ cup rice or almond milk
½ tsp. vanilla extract
1 cup fresh or frozen blueberries

①In a medium bowl stir together flours, flax seed meal, wheat germ, sucanat and salt. Set aside.
②In a small bowl or measuring cup, add mashed banana, oil, vanilla and milk.
③Add liquid ingredients to the dry. Mix until the dry ingredients are just moistened. If it is too dry, add in a little more rice milk.
④Add in baking powder and stir quickly to combine. Fold in blueberries. Fill muffin liners nearly full. Sprinkle with date sugar (optional). Bake in preheated 350* oven until toothpick inserted in center comes out clean--20-25 minutes.

Variation: For Banana Poppy seed muffins use 3 ripe, mashed bananas and 1 Tbsp. poppy seeds instead of the blueberries.

Pancakes

½ cup spelt flour
½ cup whole wheat flour
2 Tbsp. wheat germ
1 Tbsp. raw sugar
¼ tsp. salt
2 Tbsp. rice milk powder
1 ½ tsp. Ener-G Egg Replacer
½ -1 ripe banana, mashed
2 Tbsp. walnut oil
1 cup water

①Heat pan or griddle to medium-high heat.
②Combine flours, wheat germ, sugar, salt, milk powder and egg replacer in a bowl and stir to combine.
③In a small bowl, combine mashed banana, oil and water.
④Combine liquid ingredients to the dry ingredients and mix well.
⑤Ladle batter onto hot griddle. Serve with pure maple syrup or diced or pureed fruits.

Variation: Add ½ cup frozen blueberries or fruit of your choice folded into the batter.

Carob Creamy & Fruit Parfait

Carob Creamy:

½ cup millet
2 cups water
1 can coconut milk
1 cup rice or nut milk
½ cup vegan carob chips
¼ cup carob powder
2 Tbsp. molasses
1 tsp. vanilla

①Rinse millet and place in pot with the water. Bring to a boil then reduce to a simmer. Allow to simmer about 50 minutes until millet is soft and water is absorbed.
②In a saucepan, heat the coconut and rice or nut milks.
③Add in the carob chips, carob powder and molasses. Stir over medium heat until the carob chips are melted.
④Place mixture in blender with the cooked millet and add in the vanilla. Blend until smooth. Set aside to cool.

blueberries
diced strawberries
diced kiwi
assorted fresh or frozen berries
sliced bananas
granola

Layer in individual parfait cups: carob creamy, granola, fruits of your choice. Top with cashew whip cream, if desired. Serve chilled.

Apple 'n Oats Breakfast Bars

2-3 apples, grated
½ tsp. salt
¾ cup dates, chopped
1 cup regular oats
½ cup oat flour
¼ cup brown rice flour

¼ cup chopped walnuts
2 Tbsp. walnut oil
1 ½ tsp. vanilla
¼ tsp. lemon extract
¾ cup water

①Combine all ingredients in a bowl.

②Stir together well and add more water if you need to so that it will hold together.

③Press into and oiled baking dish at bake at 350* for 25-30 minutes. When cool, cut into bars.

A.M. Apple Snack

½ cup dates, chopped
2 cups walnuts, chopped
½ cup raisins
4 apples, assorted types
¼ cup maple syrup
½ tsp. cardamom
½ tsp. coriander

①Place chopped dates, nuts and raisins in a bowl.

②Core and dice apples with or without the skin and add to bowl.

③Mix in maple syrup, cardamom and coriander.

④Stir to combine all ingredients. Cover and chill until ready to serve.

Apple Butter Bars

Apple Butter Bars

¾ cup brown rice flour
¾ cup whole wheat pastry flour
¼ tsp. sea salt
¼ cup sucanat
1 ½ cups oats
½ cup maple syrup
¼ cup walnut oil
1 tsp. Ener-G baking powder
1 ½ cups apple butter

①In a large mixing bowl, combine the flours, salt, oats, sucanat and baking powder.
②In a small bowl or measuring cup stir together the syrup and oil.
③Add the liquid ingredients to the dry mixture and stir until moistened and crumbly.
④Press half of the mixture into a greased 8 x 8 baking dish.
⑤Spread apple butter evenly on top.
⑥Then sprinkle the rest of the mixture over the apple butter, patting down lightly.
Bake at 350* for 20 minutes. Cool and cut into bars.

Oatmeal–Raisin Breakfast Patties

Oatmeal-Raisin Breakfast Patties

1 ½ cups cooked oats, completely cooled or oats cooked the day before
¼ cup maple syrup
¼ cup raisins
½ cup nuts, chopped
¼ tsp. cardamom
½ tsp. coriander
½ tsp. salt
¼ cup bread crumbs

①In a large mixing bowl, combine the oats, maple syrup, cardamom, coriander, salt, raisins and nuts.
②Add in the bread crumbs a little at a time, mixing until it holds together and patties can be formed.
③Brown on a griddle that has been greased with oil.

Poi Smoothie

1 ½ cups poi
2 bananas
¾ cup fruits (any type of fresh or frozen fruit)
1 cup orange juice
1 cup ice

Combine all ingredients in a blender and blend until smooth. Makes 2 tall servings.

Granola Mix

4 cups rolled oats
½ cup sunflower seeds
½ cup wheat germ
½ tsp. cardamom
1 tsp. coriander
1 tsp. sea salt
½ cup shredded coconut
1 cup chopped almonds
¼ cup sesame seeds
1 cup dried blueberries or diced dried apples
1 cup honey
½ cup almond or peanut butter
½ cup walnut oil
1 tsp. vanilla

①In a large mixing bowl, combine first ten ingredients and stir. Set aside.
②In a small saucepan, heat the honey, almond or peanut butter, oil and vanilla. Stir until smooth.
③Pour over dry mixture. Mix well and spread evenly in a pan. Bake at 350* for 15 minutes, then lower temperature to 185* for 30 minutes. Turn off oven and let granola continue to dry out for another hour or so. Mix granola once during baking. Store in an airtight container.

Sunset

This is actually taken approximately 100 feet from where I work. I am one of the lucky ones that get to see this every night.   In my opinion Hawaii has the best sunsets... next to Arizona.

Delights

Coconut, Nut and Date Bites
Peach Cobbler
Carob Almond Crisp
Tapioca Pudding
Carob Brownies
Lemon Decadence Dessert
Tropical Trio Haupia
Apple Tart

Peach Cobbler

Peach Cobbler

¼ cup walnut oil
½ cup nut milk
½ cup raw sugar
½ tsp. vanilla
2 tsp. Ener-G egg replacer dissolved in 2 Tbsp. Water
½ cup whole wheat pastry flour
¾ cup spelt flour
¼ tsp. salt
2 tsp. Ener-G baking powder
1-15 oz. can peaches

① Preheat oven to 350*.
② In a small mixing bowl, mix together oil, milk, sugar, vanilla and egg replacer.
③ In a separate bowl, combine remaining ingredients except peaches.
④ Add liquid ingredients to the dry mixture and quickly stir to moisten and remove lumps.
⑤ Spread batter into a 8 x 8-inch square baking dish. Spoon the peaches evenly over the batter and gently pour the peach liquid over.
⑥ Bake for 40 minutes. Serve warm with a scoop of vanilla "ice cream" if desired.

Carob Almond Crisp

¼ cup brown rice syrup
½ cup maple syrup
½ cup almond or peanut butter
½ cup vegan carob chips
1 ½ tsp. vanilla
1 ½ cup chopped almonds
6 cups crispy brown rice cereal

①In a small saucepan combine the brown rice syrup and maple syrup. Heat over medium-low until it slowly begins to boil.
②Stir in the carob chips and almond or peanut butter. Mix until it is smooth.
③Remove from heat and stir in the vanilla.
④In another bowl, combine the chopped almonds and cereal. Combine both mixtures and stir well to evenly coat the cereal.
⑤Spread into a greased 9 x 13-inch pan and bake at 325* for 15 minutes and reduce temperature to 250* for 20-30 more minutes. Cool completely before slicing into squares.

Coconut, Nut and Date Bites

1 ½ cup walnuts
½ cup oats
¾ cup dates
¾ cup sucanat
½ cup flaked coconut
¼ tsp. cardamom
½ tsp. coriander
¼ tsp. ground ginger
orange juice

①In a food processor, process the walnuts until finely ground. Remove to a mixing bowl.
②Process or chop the dates very fine and add to the bowl.
③Add in the remaining ingredients and mix well.
④Add in orange juice very little at a time until mixture holds together without being too sticky.
⑤Roll into 1-inch balls and roll in more flaked coconut.
⑥Place balls on a greased cookie pan and bake at 350* for 10 minutes. Allow balls to cool on pan before removing. Store in an airtight container.

Tapioca Pudding

2 cans coconut milk
½ cup rice or nut milk
½ cup maple syrup
¼ cup honey
½ cup medium-sized tapioca pearls
¼ tsp. salt
1 tsp. vanilla

①In a saucepan, combine the coconut milk, rice or nut milk, maple syrup and honey. Bring to a low boil over medium heat.
②Add in the tapioca. Allow to simmer until pearls are clear. Stirring occasionally.
③Add in the vanilla and stir. Serve warm or chill in individual serving dishes. Garnish with mint leaves.

Carob Brownies

1 ½ cups whole wheat pastry flour
½ cup carob powder
1 cup sucanat
½ tsp. sea salt
1 cup rice milk
¼ cup walnut oil
1 Tbsp. lemon juice
1 tsp. vanilla
2 tsp. Ener-G baking powder
1 cup walnuts, chopped

①Preheat oven to 350*.
②Lightly grease 8 x 8-inch square baking pan.
③In a bowl, mix flour, carob powder, sucanat and salt together.
④In a large measuring cup, combine the milk, oil, lemon juice and vanilla.
⑤Combine the liquid and dry ingredients, mixing thoroughly to remove lumps.
⑥Add in the baking powder and nuts and quickly stir to combine.
⑦Promptly pour into baking pan and bake for 25-30 minutes.

Lemon Decadence

Lemon Decadence

1 cup oat flour (blend regular oats to make oat flour)
½ cup whole wheat pastry flour
3 Tbsp. wheat germ
½ cup walnuts, finely ground
½ tsp. cardamom
1 tsp. coriander
1 tsp. salt
¼ cup walnut oil
¼ cup maple syrup

①Preheat oven to 350*.
②Combine all of the above ingredients in a bowl and mix well.
③Press mixture into the bottom of a springform pan and bake for 10 minutes or until lightly browned. Set aside to cool.

¾ cup raw millet
3 cups water
½ cup raw cashews
½ cup lemon juice
½ cup maple syrup
¼ tsp. maple flavoring
½ tsp. lemon extract
2 tsp. vanilla extract
2 Tbsp. plain unflavored Emes gel dissolved in ½ cup hot water

①Cook millet in water until millet is soft and all the water is absorbed.
②In a blender, combine remaining ingredients with the cooked millet and blend until smooth.
③Pour into the prepared crust. Cool, then refrigerate. Allow it to set for a few hours or overnight before serving. Top with fruit or spread of your choice.

Tropical Trio Haupia

Tropical Trio Haupia
A coconut dessert

6 Tbsp. cornstarch
6 Tbsp. raw sugar
3 cups coconut milk

①Combine cornstarch with a little of the milk.
②Pour the remaining milk into a saucepan along with the sugar. Bring to a low boil.
③Once it begins to boil, slowly stir in the cornstarch and milk mixture. Continue to stir until thickened.
④When it has thickened, remove from heat and spread evenly into a 9 x 13-inch dish. Proceed with the next layer.

6 Tbsp. cornstarch
6 Tbsp. raw sugar
1 ¼ cups mango puree
1 ¾ cups coconut milk

①Combine the mango puree and coconut milk and proceed with the same steps as the original recipe.
②Spread onto the coconut layer. Allow to cool and go on to the last layer.

7 Tbsp. cornstarch
6 Tbsp. raw sugar
3 cups coconut milk
1- 8 oz. can crushed pineapple, drained

①Combine cornstarch and a small amount of the milk, set aside.
②Pour remaining milk into saucepan along with the sugar and bring to a boil.
③When it begins to boil, add in the crushed pineapple and return to a boil.
④Slowly add in the cornstarch and milk mixture, stirring until it thickens. Spread over mango layer. Cool thoroughly before covering. Chill for at least a few hours before slicing into squares and serving.

Apple Tart

Apple Tart

Crust:
2 cups whole wheat pastry flour, sifted
1 tsp. salt
¼ cup rice or almond milk
½ cup walnut oil

①In a bowl, combine all ingredients for the crust and mix well. Press into the bottom and ½-inch up the sides of a tart pan or spring form pan. Set aside.

6 to 8 granny smith apples
¼ cup sucanat
1 tsp. cinnamon
pinch of nutmeg
apricot glaze

②Peel apples, then cut in half from stem to bottom. Remove core without breaking halves. Then slice halves as thin as possible .
③Mix together the sucanat, cinnamon, and nutmeg. Sprinkle half of the sucanat mixture on the crust. Layer the apples from outside-in and work towards the center.
④Dust tart with the remaining sucanat mixture and bake at 400 degrees until the edges of apples turn brown, approximately 15 minutes.
⑤Cool, then apply glaze with a pastry brush. -- If glaze is too thick, place apricot preserve in a saucepan and add water a little at a time to thin it out.

Puohokamoa Falls

Just one of Maui's breath-taking waterfalls.   It is a 200-foot waterfall that cascades into a pool below and can only be spotted when traveling by foot along the famous coast to Hana.

Glossary

Achiote or Annatto- These are the seeds from the pod of the tree. It is dried and then infused with oil to add color and a distinctive flavor to many dishes. Goes best with tomato-based dishes. Can be found in Latin American food markets or in the Oriental section of most grocers.

Almond Butter- Just like peanut butter. Raw or roasted nuts are then ground. Very high in protein and calcium.

Arborio Rice (Riso)- High-starch kernels of this Italian-grown grain is shorter and fatter than any other short-grain rice. Arborio is traditionally used for risotto because its increased starch lends this classic dish its requisite creamy texture.

Bean Thread Noodle- Made from the Mung bean, this transparent noodle is sold in dry bundles and must be soaked in hot water before use. Found in Oriental food markets or the Oriental section of most grocers.

Brown Rice Flour- Brown rice flour has a slightly sweet flavor and its texture can be somewhat crumbly in baked goods. Best to combine brown rice flour with other types of flours in baking.

Brown Rice Syrup- Made from malted brown rice. Found in natural food markets.

Bulgur- Is a quick-cooking form of whole wheat that has been cleaned, parboiled, dried, ground into particles and sifted into distinct sizes. Four distinct grind sizes as well as whole kernel provide different textures and cooking properties for a variety of food applications. The result is a nutritious, versatile wheat product with a pleasant, nut-like flavor and an extended shelf-life that allows it to be stored for long periods.

Carob- Low in fat and calories and does not contain caffeine, methylxanthines, tannins or theobromines as chocolate does, it is a nice substitute. Naturally sweet and rich in calcium, it also aids in digestion. Use carob powder or carob chips to make healthful "chocolaty" drinks and desserts. Can be found in natural food markets.

Cashews- Lower in fat than most other nuts, this versatile nut can be used as a base to make milks, creams, dressings and desserts.

Couscous- A type of pasta made from semolina flour or whole wheat. A staple of the Northwest African countries, cooks very quickly and goes well with many types of main dishes due to its subtle flavor.

Dates- This fruit can be eaten as is or can be used to sweeten smoothies or desserts. You can purchase dates pitted. It can also be made into date butter by softening with hot water and blending until smooth and used in baked goods or as a spread. Or it can be dried and pulverized to make date sugar and be used in recipes. Date butter and date sugar can be purchased in natural food markets if you choose not to make it yourself.

Emes Kosher Jel- Contains carageenan and locust bean gum and is a vegan product. Must be dissolved in hot liquid to use to thicken desserts and make it "set." Comes unflavored or sweetened and flavored as in dessert gelatin. Can be found in specialty stores, some natural food markets or can be ordered from Country Life Natural Foods. 1-800-456-7694.

Ener-G Baking Powder- This baking powder is made with calcium carbonate and citric acid does not contain the harmful characteristics as regular baking powder or soda does. Used in place of regular baking powder or sodas, using twice as much as called for and mix it in immediately prior to baking. Can be purchased in most natural food markets.

Ener-G Egg Replacer- From the same company that makes the baking powder. Made from potato starch, tapioca, leavening and carbohydrate gum, it is a vegan product. For one egg, use 1 ½ tsp. To 2 Tbsp. water, whisking until thoroughly mixed and frothy. Available in natural food markets.

Flax Seed-The most universal function of flax seed is to produce linseed oil, this tiny seed contains several essential nutrients including calcium, iron, niacin, phosphorous and vitamin E. It's also a rich source of Omega-3 fatty acids.

Gluten-Viewed alone, gluten is a tough, elastic, grayish substance resembling chewing gum. It's the gluten in flour that, when dough is kneaded, helps hold in the gas bubbles formed by the leavening agent.

Hoisin-This thick, reddish-brown sauce is sweet and spicy, and widely used in Chinese cooking. It's a mixture of soybeans, garlic, chili peppers and various spices.

Kim Chee- A favorite side dish made with nappa cabbage and seasonings is more like a condiment. Originating in Korea, you can find it in Oriental markets and most grocers in the refrigerated section. Its degree of spiciness ranges from mild to extreme fire.

Liquid Aminos- Made from soybeans and water, used as a condiment and to add flavor to other dishes.

Masa- Cornmeal ground very fine. Easy to use and cooks quickly. Found in the Hispanic section of most grocers.

Millet- A very small pellet-like grain that can be used many ways. It can be cooked as a cereal just like oatmeal or used to make meatless meatballs or patties and also in dessert recipes when blended. It is well tolerated by individuals who have wheat or other kinds of food allergies.

Nut Milk- Nearly any type of nut makes good nut milk. Liquefy in a blender ½ cup nuts to 1 quart of water. Add dates or honey to desired sweetness. A small pinch of salt and 1 teaspoon of vanilla, if desired. Keeps in refrigerator for up to 3 days.

Nutritional Yeast- A food yeast not to be confused with Brewer's yeast. Nutritional yeast is high in B vitamins and has a "cheesy" flavor. Find it in the bulk section of natural food stores.

Orzo- Type of pasta

Pimientos- Sweet red bell peppers are roasted to make pimientos. Can be found in cans or small jars usually in the canned vegetable aisle of grocery stores.

Quinoa-Tiny and bead-shaped, the ivory-colored quinoa cooks like rice (taking half the time of regular rice) and expands to four times its original volume. To this day it's an important food in South American cuisine. Hailed as the "super grain of the future," quinoa contains more protein than any other grain.

Sea Salt- We prefer to use Celtic Sea Salt because of the many health benefits derived from its use and because of its excellent flavor. It is added into dishes at the end of cooking. For all other uses where salt is needed, we use the regular sea salt found in natural food stores.

Soba- A Japanese noodle made from buckwheat. Very nutritious and delicious. It can be used for cold noodle salads or eaten hot in a broth.

Somen- Asian noodles that are made from wheat flour, it is a fine thread noodle and can be used the same way as soba (see above).

Spelt-is an ancient cereal grain that has a mellow nutty flavor. The easily digestible spelt has slightly higher protein content than wheat and can be tolerated by those with wheat allergies

Sucanat- A brand of evaporated cane juice that is more nutritious as a sweetener alternative to refined or raw sugar. Another brand name is Rapadura.

Tahini- A paste made from grinding sesame seeds. Used traditionally in Mid-Eastern dishes. Available in natural food markets. Refrigerate after opening.

Thai Curry Paste- Comes in yellow, green or red curry paste. It is added in small amounts to a coconut milk base as it is very spicy. The more you add, the spicier your final dish will be. Found in Oriental food markets or the Oriental section of most grocers.

Thai Sweet Chili Sauce- A condiment used as a dipping sauce for spring rolls and other foods, it can also be used to add an interesting flavor to salad dressings.

Udon- Asian noodle made from wheat flour that is thick and generally eaten in a broth with vegetables.

Vegetable Bouillon- Made from herbs, you can find vegan vegetable bouillon at the natural foods market.

Vermicelli-Type of pasta resembling thin, threadlike strands.

Wasabi- Oriental condiment made from horseradish, it is very spicy and in general used mixed with soy sauce for dipping Japanese *sushi*.

Wheat Germ- The heart of the wheat berry. High in dietary fiber and provides folic acid, phosphorus, magnesium, zinc, vitamin E and thiamin. It has a delicious nutty flavor that is delicious added to baked goods, cooked oatmeal, etc.

Whole Wheat Pastry Flour-typically mixed with all-purpose or bread flour to make bread or baked goods.

Yam Noodle-Alimentary paste made from yam flour, calcium hydroxide water.Tradtionally used in sukiyaki

"Remember that when you eat flesh meat, you are but eating grains and vegetables secondhand; for the animal receives from these things the nutrition that makes it grow and prepares it for market. The life that was in the grains and vegetables passes into the animal, and becomes part of its life, and then human beings eat the animal. Why are they so willing to eat their food secondhand?"

"In the beginning, fruit was pronounced by God as "good for food." The permission to eat flesh meat was a consequence of the fall. Not till after the flood man was given permission to eat the flesh animals. Why, then, need we eat flesh meat? Few who eat this know how full it is of disease. Flesh meat never was the best food, and now it is cursed by disease."

"The thought of killing animals to be eaten is in itself revolting. If man's natural sense had not been perverted by the indulgence of appetite, human beings would not think of eating the flesh of animals."

"The world had become so corrupt through indulgence of appetite and debased passion in the days of Noah that God destroyed its inhabitants by the waters of the Flood. And as men again multiplied upon the earth the indulgence in wine to intoxication perverted the senses and prepared the way for excessive meat eating and the strengthening of the animal passions. Men lifted themselves up against the God of heaven; and their faculties and opportunities were devoted to glorifying themselves rather than honoring their Creator."

"The word of God plainly warns us that unless we abstain from fleshly lusts, the physical nature will be brought into conflict with the spiritual nature. Lustful eating wars against health and peace. Thus a warfare is instituted between the higher and the lower attributes of the man. The lower propensities, strong and active, oppress the soul. The highest interests of the being are imperiled by the indulgence of appetites unsanctioned by Heaven."

My wife Crystal and I will jump at the chance to tell any willing ear about health reform. Utilizing my talent for cooking is where I can do that best. And because I like my food to be fun as well as explosive (kind of how I am). I am always trying to push the scale of creativity, making health reform exciting. This is the reason why we decided to create this cookbook. Use this book as a jumping board into a world of healthful living, and don't stop there. Constantly seek to improve your lifestyle by doing what is right in the eyes of the lord, the blessings will be yours. "Or do you not know that your body is the temple of the Holy Spirit who is in you, whom you have from God, and you are not your own? For you were bought with a price; therefore glorify god in your body and in your spirit, which are God's 1 Corinthians 6:19, 20